If you haven't had your life what have you had?

—Henry James

This book is dedicated to those who live in the moment, who are committed to living their lives on purpose.

ACKNOWLEDGEMENTS
These quotations were gathered lovingly but unscientifically over several years and/or contributed by many friends or acquaintances. Some arrived—and survived in our files—on scraps of paper and may therefore be imperfectly worded or attributed. To the authors, contributors and original sources, our thanks, and where appropriate, our apologies. —The Editors

WITH SPECIAL THANKS TO
Jason Aldrich, Gloria Austin, Gerry Baird, Jay Baird, Neil Beaton, Josie Bissett, Laura Boro, Chris Dalke, Jim and Alyssa Darragh & Family, Jennifer and Matt Ellison & Family, Rob Estes, Michael and Leianne Flynn & Family, Sarah Forster, Jennifer Hurwitz, Heidi Jones, Carol Anne Kennedy, June Martin, Jessica Phoenix and Tom DesLongchamp, Janet Potter & Family, Diane Roger, Kirsten and Garrett Sessions, Kristel Wills, Clarie Yam and Erik Lee, Heidi Yamada & Family, Justi and Tote Yamada & Family, Bob and Val Yamada, Kaz and Kristin Yamada & Family, Tai and Joy Yamada, Anne Zadra, August and Arline Zadra, Dan Zadra, and Gus and Rosie Zadra.

CREDITS
Compiled by Kobi Yamada
Designed by Steve Potter & Jenica Wilkie

ISBN: 978-1-932319-00-2

6th Printing. 10K 06 08   Printed in China

Oh, the experience of this sweet life. —Dante

Life is here and it is now…either we meet it, we live it or we miss it. All life resides in the narrow margin and the broad expanse of the moment. It is in the doing, the dreaming, the feeling and the caring. It is always present in a glorious attempt, a lofty dream, a brilliant insight, an irreplaceable experience, a calming breath, an unbelievable feeling and an irrepressible passion.

An unlived life is littered with "could haves," "should haves" and "if onlys." Each moment greets us full of possibility and leaves us hoping we are better for having met. While it is true that we only have right now, there will never be a time when it's not now. Grandma Moses said it best, "Life is what we make it, always has been and always will be."

bepresent.

In life,
there are no
ordinary
moments.
Most of us
never really
recognize
the most
significant
moments of our lives
when they're
happening.

—Kathleen Magee

befirst.

To achieve the impossible, it is precisely the unthinkable that must be thought.

—Tom Robbins

bedaring.

If you're looking for a big opportunity, seek out a big problem.

—H. Jackson Brown, Jr.

beproactive.

Whatever you are meant to do, move toward it and it will come to you.

—Gloria Dunn

beconstructive.

Clear your mind of can't.

—Samuel Johnson

beresourceful.

Almost everything comes from almost nothing.

—Henri-Frédéric Amiel

beexcited.

The minute you begin to do what you really want to do, it's really a different kind of life.

—Buckminster Fuller

bebrilliant.

Do more than exist,
live.
Do more than touch,
feel.
Do more than look,
observe.
Do more than read,
absorb.
Do more than hear,
listen.
Do more than listen,
understand.
Do more than think,
ponder.
Do more than talk,
say something.

—John H. Rhoades

beamazed.

As I started looking, I found more and more.

—Valerie Steele

beamazing.

It is up to you to illuminate the world.

—Phillippe Venier

beready.

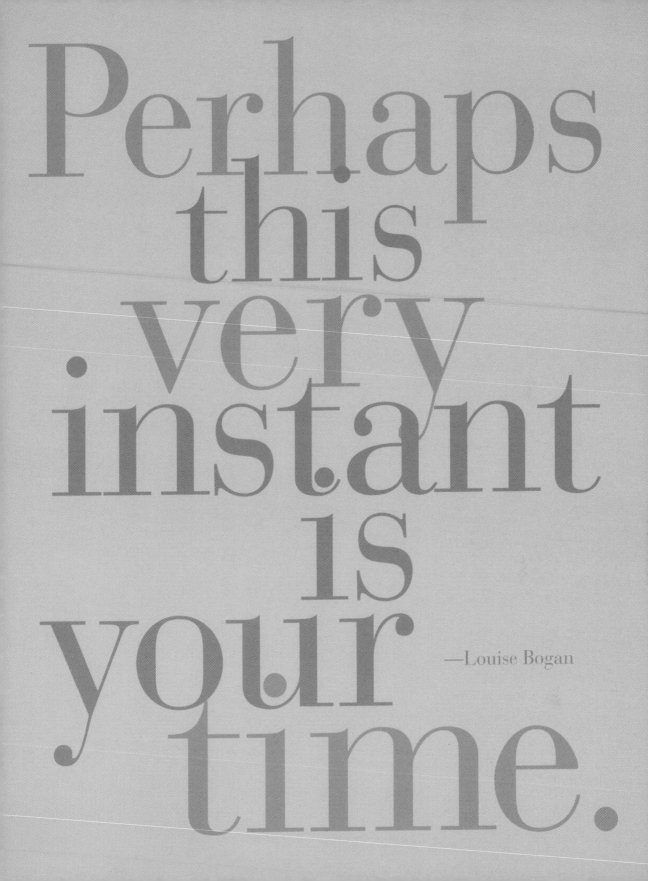

Perhaps this very instant is your time.

—Louise Bogan

bestrong.

We define ourselves by the best that is in us, not the worst that has been done to us.

—Edward Lewis

becommitted.

From a certain point onward there is no longer any turning back. That is the point that must be reached.

—Franz Kafka

beunstoppable.

After the
final no
there comes
a yes,
and on
that yes
the future
world
depends.

—Wallace Stevens

beboundless.

There are some people who live in a dream world, and there are some who face reality; and then there are those who turn one into the other.

—Douglas Everett

bedifferent.

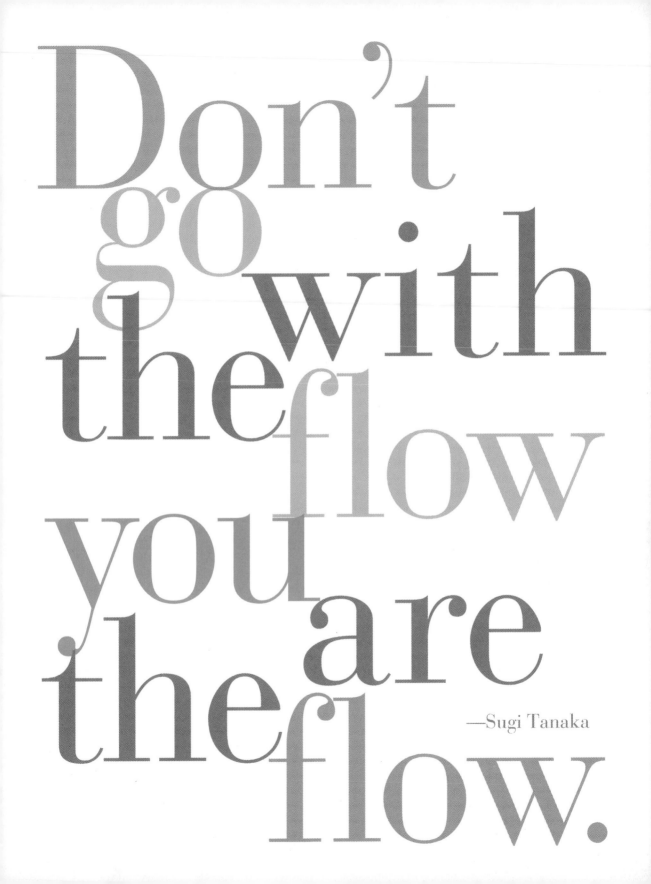

Don't go with the flow you are the flow.

—Sugi Tanaka

bealive.

The purpose of life is to live it, to taste experience to the utmost, to reach out eagerly and without fear for newer and richer experience.

—Eleanor Roosevelt

bemoved.

Live to the point of tears.

—Albert Camus

besincere.

I am
seeking,
I am striving,
I am in it with
all my
heart.

—Vincent van Gogh

bethere.

God calls you to the place where your deep gladness and the world's deep hunger meet.

—Frederick Buechner

beinspired.

The soul has greater need of the ideal than the real. It is by the real that we exist, it is by the ideal that we live.

—Victor Hugo

bepassionate.

Whatever comes from the **heart** carries the heat and color of its birthplace.

—Oliver Wendell Holmes, Sr.

bepositive.

What you find in your mind is what you put there. Put good things in there.

—Mary Ford

beresilient.

There is nothing we can't live down, rise above or overcome.

—Ella Wheeler Wilcox

bebrave.

Most of our obstacles would melt away if instead of cowering before them, we should make up our minds to walk boldly through them.

—Orison Swett Marden

behopeful.

I haven't a clue as to how my story will end. But that's all right. When you set out on a journey and night covers the road, that's when you discover the stars.

—Nancy Willard

betrue.

At the heart of each of us, whatever our imperfections, there exists a silent pulse of perfect rhythm, which is absolutely individual and unique, and yet which connects us to everything else.

—George Leonard

beinvolved.

Life is not a path of coincidence, happenstance, and luck, but rather an unexplainable, meticulously charted course for one to touch the lives of others and make a difference in the world.

—Barbara Dillinham

begood.

So act that your principle of action might safely be made law for the whole world.

—Immanuel Kant

begenerous.

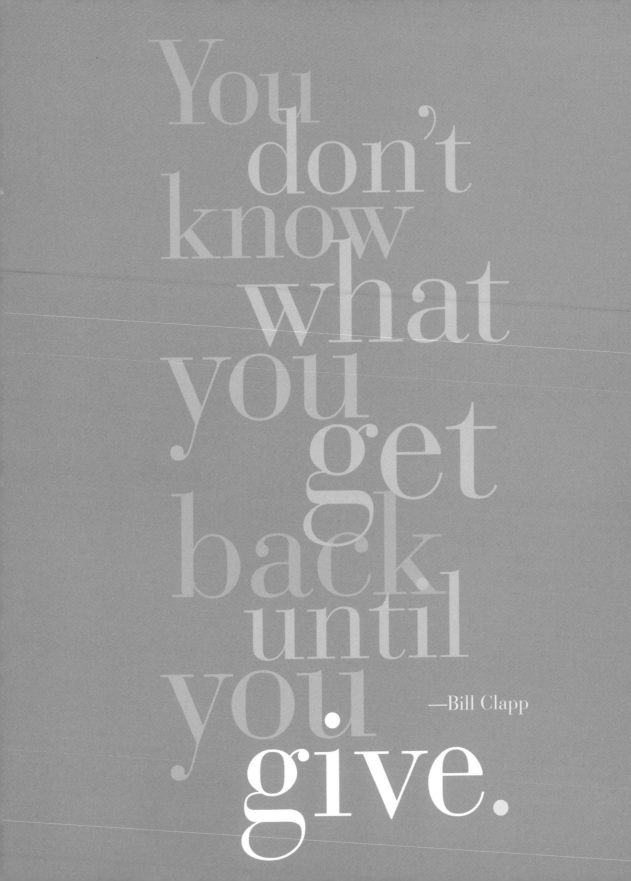

You don't know what you get back until you give.

—Bill Clapp

behumble.

Nobody can conceive or imagine all the wonders there are unseen and unseeable in the world.

—Francis P. Church

beconfident.

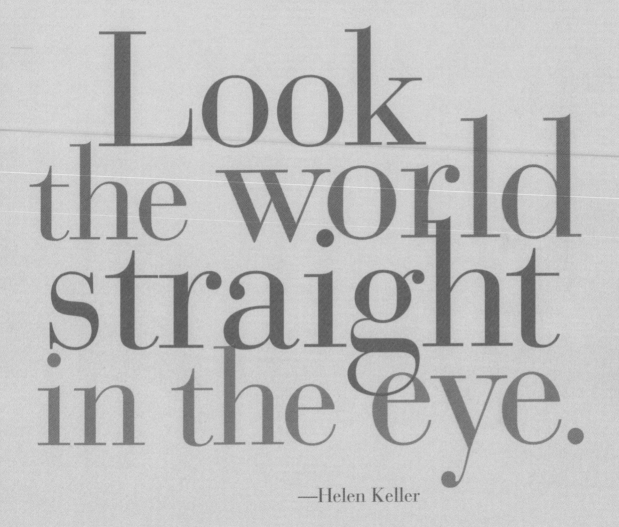

Look the world straight in the eye.

—Helen Keller

bestill.

When you become quiet, it just dawns on you.

—Thomas Edison

bereal.

The true harvest of my daily life is somewhat as intangible and indescribable as the tints of morning or evening. It is a little stardust caught, a segment of the rainbow which I have clutched.

—Henry David Thoreau

behappy.

The principal thing in this world is to keep one's soul aloft.

—Gustave Flaubert

bespontaneous.

Live nutty.
Just occasionally.
Just once in a while.
And see what happens.
It brightens
up the day.

—Leo Buscaglia

beopen.

Above all, watch with glittering eyes the whole world around you, because the greatest secrets are always hidden in the most unlikely places. Those who don't believe in magic will never find it.

—Roald Dahl

beyourself.

Simply, the thing that I am shall make me live.

—William Shakespeare